A Light in the Tunnel

A Collection of Love Poems When You're Going through Life's Transitions

Peace +
Blessings,
[signature]

Victoria TenEyck

DBP Publications

Rayville, Louisiana

Printed in the United States of America

First Printing: 2018

ISBN-13: 978-1986253611

ISBN-10: 1986253619

DBP Publications

P.O. Box 575

Rayville, Louisiana, 71269

www.refusetolose31.com

Scripture quotation was taken from www.biblegateway.com. Copyright © 2015 by The Lockman Foundation, La Habra, CA 90631. All rights reserved.

Lyrics from "Listen to your Heart" from the album Love Stories are used with permission from the artist, Frank McComb, LaVerne, California.

The picture on the back cover is used with permission from the photographer, Shelby Tuck-Horton, Mitchellville, Maryland.

At the specific preference of the author, DBP Publications allowed this work to remain exactly as the author intended, verbatim, and without editorial input.

Dedication

To God for Allowing Me
My Mom for Having Me
My Children for Keeping Me
To KP for Inspiring Me

Preface

As long as I can remember, I've always liked poems. This goes back to my childhood where I have now found composition books that held various poems and inspirational quotes that I liked from me, friends, and others. As I continue to travel on life's journey, I went back to what comforted me. These poems express love, heartache, pain, joy, sorrow, happiness, and all the range of emotions that a person can experience. Poems are important to me because they can simply tell a story. It can be a story of your feelings, your hopes, your dreams, and your desires while being authentic. Poems can help you express to someone what you really feel that you can't say to them in person. Poems can help you purge what shouldn't be in you. Poems can be liberating, but also show that you've been in bondage. The poems contained in this book are my release as I traveled through one of life's unplanned but necessary transitions. The end of one chapter in my life, the longing for someone you love, and all the emotions in between. As you may have encountered some transitions in your life, I pray that at your darkest moments, you focus on the light. I'm here to tell you that one day, it WILL BE all right! Peace and Blessing!

Table of Contents

"When you are cursed/blessed with a big heart,
life is not always fair when loving people."

—Bishop TD Jakes

SHORT CHANGED

From the series The Will to Recover

(2 Samuel 9:1–4)

LOVE

Love

What is Love?

Is it all in your mind

Is it all in your thoughts

Is it a mystery

Is it what you want it to be

It is real

The feelings that I feel

Is it lust or make-believe

Why do we love

Who we love

Do we choose or

Is it chosen for us

<u>Thinking of Love</u>

What is it?

Do you have it

Do you know what it feels like

Is it wind in your hair

Sun on your face

Eyes staring at you

Wanting to be with you

It's all that and more

What a shame if you haven't experienced it

You don't know what you're missing

What you say …

What is it?

What is Love?

What are you

Who are you

Why don't you release me

I don't want you around

You've never loved me

You've never had my back

You just make me think that you're here

You just make me think that you're real

You just make me think that you wanted me

But nothing with you is real

The Time is Now

If you are ever going to love me
Love me now while I can know.
The sweet and tender feelings
From which true affections flow
Love me now while I am living.
Do not wait till I am gone
And then have it chiseled in marble
Sweet words on ice-cold stone
If you have tender thoughts of me,
Please tell me now
If you wait until I am sleeping, never to awaken,
There will be death between us
And I won't hear you then.
So if you love me, even a little bit
Let me know it while I am living
So I can treasure it
-Anonymous

Love

Love is forgiving and forgetting,

But not regretting

Love is giving and not receiving,

Leaving and not grieving.

Love will never doubt or look for a way out

It will supply and never deny

Love is more than a kiss or a hug

Love will take the time out of a busy day

Just to help someone along the way

Love is not taught nor can be bought

Love is patience and understanding

But not demanding

Love is a gift from above

It is giving for the living

-Author Unknown

<u>Reflections</u>

Love is like a mirror

When you love another

You become their mirror

And they become yours

And reflecting each other's love

You see infinity

DREAMS

<u>Remember the Time</u>

I remember a time when you wanted me

I remember a time when you wanted the arguments to stop

And just keep loving me

I remember a time when you told me what I needed to hear

Versus what I wanted to hear

I remember a time when you wanted to be in my presence

I remember a time when you deposited nuggets in my life

Without wanting to take it back

I remember a time when you saw me for me

And accepted me just the same

But that time is gone now

Long gone but not forgotten

For You or Me

I don't know who she is

I don't know where she is

Whether she is someone in your life now

Or someone yet to come

But when you meet that one

To turn your heart around

She will be very special

That is my hope for you

And I am excited about it happening to you too

<u>Wondering</u>

Here I am, sitting on the edge of my bed, wondering

Wondering about him and if I will see him again

All I have to do is close my eyes, and I can see him

Dark skin, bald head, chiseled body

Arms strong enough to hold up the world and me in it

As I continue to think about him

I can actually smell him… ummmm

There's nothing like a good smelling man

I love his cologne, and I remember

When he first walked up behind me

Dreams

In the depth of my soul

There you are

Unnerving me

So it seems

Since fairy tales aren't true

I assume you are make-believe

Only a fantasy in my head

Is it wrong

For one to dream

Question

I think of you often and wonder

What would it have been like

Me and You

Is that so untrue

Genuineness

Everything about you is genuine

How you make me feel

How you make me smile

How you make me laugh

How you make me blush inside

I don't know how you do it

Thank you for letting me back in your world

I remember being there before

A long, long time ago

I am still comforted by your presence

You make this uptown girl feel secure

I don't know what lies ahead for this journey

But I do know

I'm enjoying every minute of it

Every Moment

I can't stop thinking about you

I can't stop thinking about us

When will I see you again

How long will it be this time

Every moment with you is like a breath of fresh air

I long to be with you

I long to smile again when I'm with you

I cherish every moment because I don't know when it will come again

Although I don't know when it will end

I'm glad that it began again

Reminiscing about the good times

And settling on the past

What will the future hold?

Anything, nothing, something

MEMORIES

I Wait for You

In my car, I wait for you
I slowly look between the houses, the cars, the trees
For just a glance
A glance of you
Your body, your presence, your smile
How come I don't see you anymore
Was it just a tease
A tease to have me come back for more
Just one more time
To please the inner me
As I wait for you

Does He Know

I wonder if he knows

If he knows what I think about him

As I see him and don't see him

All I need to do is close my eyes

Close my eyes to experience

His touch, his smell, his smile

How he caresses my hair, my shoulders, and my back

If I keep my eyes closed

Just long enough to remember

I remember his hugs, his love, and his kiss

Just long enough to give me enough to carry on

Till I see him or don't see him

And then I wonder

What does he think of me

<u>Longing</u>

Do you know what I long for

I long for you and your touch

Just one more time

Why do you tease me but don't please me

It's torturous

To be around you

Wanting you

But not having you

The Rain

Pitter Pat

Pitter Pat

As the rain begins to fall

I think of you

As the night turns the deepest blue

It's just between me and you

Our bodies hot

The night air cool

We make love till the night turns to dew

I just can't get enough of you

I Remember Us

When I close my eyes

And think of you

My body parts start to tingle

I remember your eyes, your hands, and your body

I remember how your body feels up against mine

My heart starts to beat with excitement

I see you, feel you, and need you

Up against the wall with delight

You start to kiss me

And I kissing you back

Taking me to ecstasy

As I Sleep

In the middle of the night

You come home

Off come your clothes

As you slip into bed

On top of me

You slowly wake me with delight

I feel you

You feel me

We come in delight

And we sleep all through the night

Remembrance

I miss you

I miss your walk

I miss your talk

I miss your smile

I miss how I felt when I was near you, and around you

I miss how you made me feel

How you warmed my nights and brightened my days

You were my protector

You were my security

You were my rock

I loved you

SORROW

Where Are You

Here I sit in my own misery

Missing the hell out of you, but not wanting to tell you

For the ultimate fear

Fear of the unknown

Fear of what you may not say

I miss the walk, talk, smile, face, body, and hands

I want to call you

I want to tell you I miss you

I want to tell you I love you

I want to tell you I want you in my life, but I'm scared

Why do I do this to myself

My own worst enemy

I want to just run to you, come to you, hug you, and hold you so tight

Give you all my love

Touch you so you'll know how I feel

So, as you go to bed tonight

Rest Easy

I'm thinking of you

Missing you

<u>Why</u>

Lord, please help me

Take the pain away

I don't want to feel it anymore

Especially knowing You can cure me ever more

What is it all for

What is the point

What is the purpose

I have nothing left to give

Pondering

When I look in the mirror

What do I really see

A person who can't be all that

Because if I were all that

Then someone would definitely be interested

Someone would definitely want to be around

Someone would definitely not want me out of their sight

Someone would want to hold me

And not let me go

But maybe they really see

That I'm not all what I seem to be

I Can't Have You

Why do you continue to be around me

You know I can't have you

Nor you having me

Circumstances haven't changed

Still in the same dull drum

As my heart beats for another

Knowing that it's you that I want

I'll continue to just dream and wonder

As you satisfy me, my body, and my psyche

Untouched Love

What do you do when you love someone

But can't have them

How many times do you think about them

As they dance through your thoughts

Do you remember the last time you looked into each other's eyes

The last time you held their hand and felt

The warmth of their body

What do you do when you can't have them

How it aches to know you'll never again be with them

Not now, not ever, not this lifetime

Inner Struggle

There is not a day that goes by that I don't think about you

Why do I put myself through this torture

Do you love me

Do you like me

Did you ever care

Those that know you are in your corner

But I can't seem to shake you

Out of my mind, body, and soul

I ask and beg God to remove you

But there you are

And I'm still here

Alone and wondering when will it end

Fear

My everlasting friend

The one who is always there for me

The one who never leaves my side

What would I do without you

We've become fond of one another

You seem so right for me

Although I'm told you're all wrong for me

People want me to push you away

How could that be

You've comforted me all along

I may not know how to love without you

But I'll try

If it will help me to

Never want to give up and die

Untitled

In the depth of my soul, I long for you

I wonder where you are as my world gets darker and darker

I can't see you

I don't know where you are

At times, I feel you

Feel you around me, surrounding me with your love

You are so close, yet so far away

When will I meet you, or

Have you always been there

Rain Rain Go Away

In the middle of the night
I hear you
Pitter pat pitter pat
As I listen to myself breathing
As I feel my heart beating
Where am I
Who am I really
Where do I want to be
Who do I want to be with
Calgon, take me away
I don't like this place
I don't like this space
By myself, lonely and thinking
Even the raindrops have each other
But who do I have
What do I have
Just the memories of you

You Didn't Know

In the depth of the soul

I am alive

I love music

I love dance

I love to be loved

On the outside, I am the walking dead

Playing the game like it's supposed to be played

Dutiful wife

Loving mother

But dead inside

Those around me say they love me

But they really don't know me

If they did

They would know how to tap into me

Instead, they see me but don't see me

I'm dying inside

And at what cost

Mine

My life

My happiness

My tears

Come Out

Why am I thinking of you

When you probably aren't thinking of me

Did you ever know how I really felt?

Inside my heart

My feelings were real

It's hard to accept

That it's not you; it's me

That blocks my happiness

Darkness

Darkness surrounds me

Surrounds me wherever I go

Skeleton, empty bones

No flesh, no muscle, just bones

Why Am I Here?

This is a dark, lonely place

A place only you can go

No one is here for you

Nobody has to know

Pain, hurt, confusion

Is all that you see and hear

Heartache, headache, heaviness

Is all that it seems to be

I Don't Know

What seems like a lifetime

Recalling the day and time when you decided to let me go

Some say it's for the good

And that it will make me grow

However, they will never really know

My love for you runs deep

My feelings for you were true

However, now, I will never really know

Did you ever really love me?

Did you ever really care?

Or was I just something that you just decided to bear

I still believe and always will do

The cross in our path was purposeful too

That leap in my spirit connected us too

But now I really don't know what I should actually do

I wait for your call

And to see your face too

But was it all make-believe

As I continue to dream of you

Should I trust my feelings

Should I listen to thee

As all of this has me asking

Was it just only me

LIGHT

Thinking

Each Moment in Time

Is a Chance to Hope

To Dream

And to Begin Again

Listen to your heart

Your heart is never wrong

Always face the truth

Your heart will lead you on

—Lyrics from "Listen To Your Heart"

From the album LOVE STORIES

Frank McComb

Aspirations

No matter how hard you try to run

From what God has already appointed

Your heart wants what it wants

And it can be said it's already done

You're just players in this play

Trying to catch up to the storyline

Don't lie to yourself

You need to free yourself

So Dream without Fear

And Love without Limits

Hey You

Just wanted to say hello

Feeling hopeful

Feel blessed to know that you're out there too

You're out there waiting for me

You're out there hoping for me

You're out there wondering where I am

Well I'm here

I'm here getting myself together for you

Going through some ups and downs

Trying to make myself true—for you

You are who I want

You are what I want

You are who I long for

Can't wait to meet you

Can't wait to see you

So you can have all of me

Clean, unadulterated me

Who God made me to be—for you

So I wait…

Patiently…

To see you

To love you

To be with you

Always

Hey You

The Ultimate Love

1 Corinthians 13:4–8

Amplified Bible (AMP)

"4 Love endures with patience and serenity, love is kind and thoughtful, and is not jealous or envious; love does not brag and is not proud or arrogant. 5 It is not rude; it is not self-seeking, it is not provoked [nor overly sensitive and easily angered]; it does not take into account a wrong endured. 6 It does not rejoice at injustice, but rejoices with the truth [when right and truth prevail]. 7 Love bears all things [regardless of what comes], believes all things [looking for the best in each one], hopes all things [remaining steadfast during difficult times], endures all things [without weakening].8 Love never fails [it never fades nor ends]."

Dear God

Here I come to You again
Wondering if I can return to You
Humbled, yet ashamed
Covering my face, head bowed
Not sure if You'll let me in
Been gone for some time now
I finally get it
I can't do ANYTHING without You
With You, there is Peace
With You, there is Calm
With You, there is No Condemnation
With You, there is LOVE
With You, there is Acceptance
When all else before have failed
Sex, drugs, alcohol
Fake relationships
Negative self-talk
You were just waiting on me
You were there all along
When I couldn't even see
How Loving and PATIENT You are
To love me with all my flaws
Is it You who made me

Is it You who purposed me

Glad to RETURN to You

In Your open arms

I will not let You down this time

I am here for good

To be what You CREATED ME to be

To fulfill my PURPOSE

To really know what TRUE LOVE is

You are truly my FATHER

I thank You for the lessons

No matter how painful and challenging they may have been

It was all worth it

To get me to this point

To return back into Your loving arms

I can now see You in EVERYTHING

In the good, the bad, and the uncertainty

I can hear more of You

I can see more of You in others

I patiently wait

As my life unfolds

Not knowing what it will bring

But can rest easy now

Knowing that YOU are in CONTROL

Yes, I Can

2 Corinthians 12:8–10

Amplified Bible (AMP)

"8 Concerning this I pleaded with the Lord three times that it might leave me; 9 but He has said to me, 'My grace is sufficient for you [My lovingkindness and My mercy are more than enough—always available—regardless of the situation]; for [My] power is being perfected [and is completed and shows itself most effectively] in [your] weakness.' Therefore, I will all the more gladly boast in my weaknesses, so that the power of Christ [may completely enfold me and] may dwell in me. 10 So I am well pleased with weaknesses, with insults, with distresses, with persecutions, and with difficulties, for the sake of Christ; for when I am weak [in human strength], then I am strong [truly able, truly powerful, truly drawing from God's strength]."